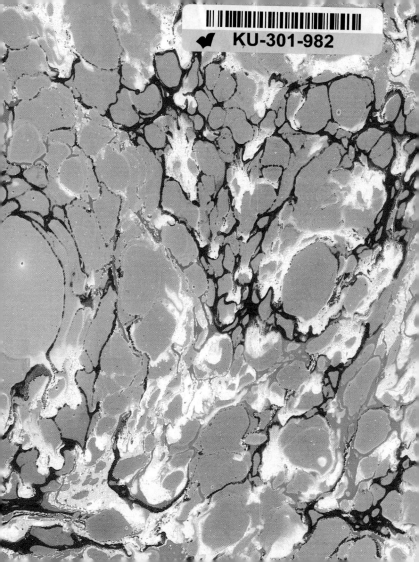

THE NATIONAL TRUST
Little Library

Pasta

JILL NORMAN

DORLING KINDERSLEY
LONDON

A DORLING KINDERSLEY BOOK

EDITOR LAURA HARPER

SENIOR EDITOR CAROLYN RYDEN

DESIGN MATHEWSON BULL

PHOTOGRAPHER DAVE KING

FIRST PUBLISHED IN GREAT BRITAIN IN 1990 BY
DORLING KINDERSLEY LIMITED
9 HENRIETTA STREET, LONDON WC2E 8PS

BRITISH LIBRARY CATALOGUING IN PUBLICATION DATA

NORMAN, JILL
PASTA
I. FOOD: PASTA DISHES – RECIPES
I. TITLE II. SERIES
641.822

ISBN 0-86318-488-X

PRINTED AND BOUND IN HONG KONG
BY IMAGO

CONTENTS

INTRODUCTION

$\mathscr{P}$ASTA AND NOODLES – *the name varies with the country of origin* – *are made from flour mixed with a liquid, usually egg or water. Flavourings or colourings, such as spinach, herbs, tomato purée, olives or cuttlefish ink, are sometimes added to the basic dough. This is kneaded, rolled, cut, perhaps stuffed, then boiled, steamed, baked or fried, and served with a sauce or in a broth.*

Pasta has its roots in many cultures. The Etruscans and ancient Greeks ate pasta and had special implements to shape it; Apicius, the Roman gourmet, included it in his De Re Coquinaria (On Cookery). *Several centuries later the Arabs took pasta from the eastern Mediterranean to Spain.*

Long before Marco Polo made his journey across Asia, noodles were a staple of the diet there. They were street food, the basic everyday food of the poor, but also appeared at banquets as a symbol of longevity. As the Mongols moved west in the 13th century they took their stuffed pasta and small dumplings across Siberia.

The stuffed pasta of Asia and Europe is all made in a similar way. Triangles, crescents, squares and circles are filled with a variety of foods and then fried, baked or boiled.

Chinese wontons, filled with pork or prawns, are served in a broth or deep fried as a snack. Mongol pel'meni spread west from Siberia and today are popular everywhere in the Soviet Union. In the Ukraine they are called vareniki; *in Armenia (and Turkey)* mantı. *The* kreplachs *of the central European Jews are closely related to pel'meni, and to the* pierogi *of Polish cooking. They are served in soup or fried in chicken fat to accompany a meat dish.*

Undeniably the Italians have the greatest variety of all forms of pasta and even more names. In the 14th century Francesco Datini, the Merchant of Prato, wrote in his private papers of ravioli being served as a delicacy at the first course of a banquet. They were stuffed with ground pork, eggs, cheese, a little sugar and parsley,

Italian pasta label

then fried and served powdered with sugar. Bartolomeo Scappi's great cookery book of 1570 has recipes for tagliatelle and maccheroni cooked in broth or milk and served with cinnamon and sugar. By this time pasta was available commercially, but was expensive. The guild of pasta makers, the vermicellai, now demanded the sole right to make pasta and guarded their trade jealously from the bakers. Pasta shops proliferated throughout Italy. By 1785 there were 280 in Naples; the streets were full of racks of pasta drying in the hot wind, and of maccheroni sellers cooking on street corners. By the 19th century Naples had a huge pasta industry, and the thousands of emigrants who sailed for the United States took their staple food with them, thus ensuring its continued popularity across the Atlantic.

FRESH PASTA

*I*T IS QUITE EASY *to make fresh pasta at home – see p. 24 – and well worth the effort. The basic form for every variety is the* sfoglia, *a sheet of dough, which is cut to ribbons of varying width, or into the large squares or rounds used for filled pasta.*

The dried pasta shapes of commerce come in several colours, but the black pasta made with the ink of cuttlefish is only obtainable fresh.

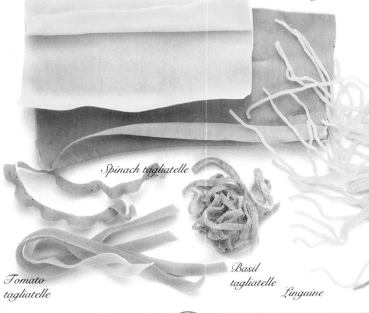

Lasagne and lasagne verdi

Spinach tagliatelle

Tomato tagliatelle

Basil tagliatelle

Linguine

6

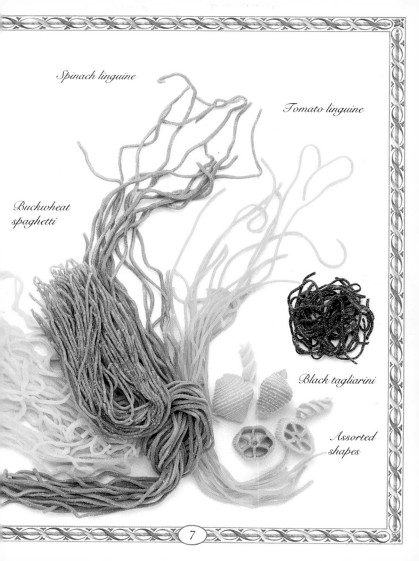

Spinach linguine

Tomato linguine

Buckwheat spaghetti

Black tagliarini

Assorted shapes

RIBBONS & STICKS

*F*LAT PASTA *is usually made with egg. Under American food law, the definition of any commercial product called 'noodles' specifies the use of egg. Fresh egg pasta is lighter and more delicate than the dried version, and amply repays the effort of making it at home (see the instructions on p. 24). A flat sheet of dough is cut into the required shapes: wide for lasagne, ribbons for fettuccine and tagliatelle, and fine strands for linguine.*

Lasagne and lasagne verdi

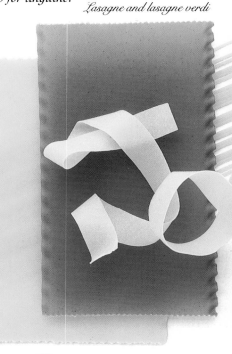

Wholewheat spaghetti is an invention of health food commercialism, not much favoured in Italy where everybody knows that pasta is neither fattening nor likely to cause any other problems.

Spaghetti

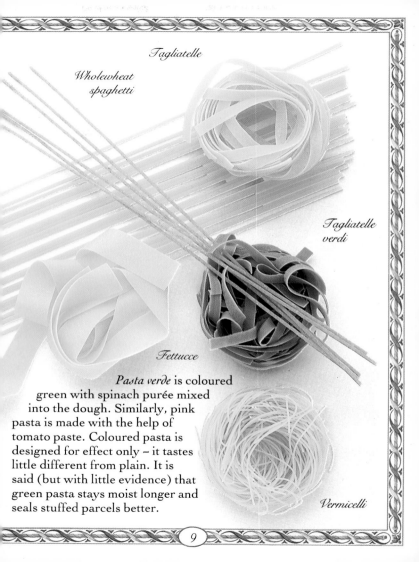

Tagliatelle

*Wholewheat
spaghetti*

*Tagliatelle
verdi*

Fettucce

Pasta verde is coloured
green with spinach purée mixed
into the dough. Similarly, pink
pasta is made with the help of
tomato paste. Coloured pasta is
designed for effect only – it tastes
little different from plain. It is
said (but with little evidence) that
green pasta stays moist longer and
seals stuffed parcels better.

Vermicelli

TUBES

The TWO PRINCIPAL *ways of cooking pasta are boiling or baking. Baked pasta* (pasta al forno) *is usually made either with large flat sheets of egg pasta* (lasagne) *alternating with a thick sauce of vegetables or meat, or by stuffing one of the tubular shapes* (tufoli, rigatoni, *and the most famous of them all,* cannelloni). *The stuffed shapes are then covered with more of the sauce, or with a different sauce, and baked in the oven. Smaller tubes may be baked in a sauce as a gratin.*

Rigatoni

Elbow macaroni

The dried pasta shapes of commerce are made of a very hard grain called durum wheat, ground to an amber flour called *semola* or *semolina* in Italian, which can be confusing in English: be sure to ask for *semolina flour*, not just *semolina*. Fresh pasta can be made with strong bread flour or with unbleached plain flour.

Maccheroncelli

Ziti (bridegrooms)

Penne (quills)

Occhi di lupo (wolf's eyes)

Cannelloni

SMALL SHAPES

*T*HERE IS AN ENDLESS VARIETY *of very small shapes of pasta, collectively known as* pastina, *ranging from solid little blobs called* orzo *(barley) or* semi *(seeds) to more fanciful miniature shapes. These are given to children or used in light broths topped with a little grated cheese.*

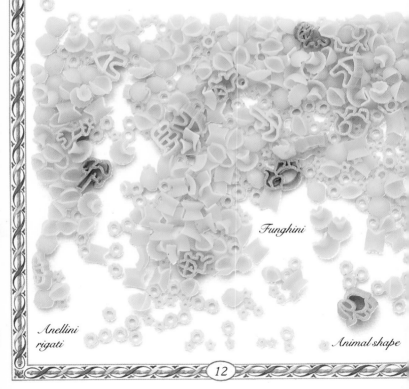

Funghini

Anellini rigati

Animal shape

Soups destined to serve as a main course, such as min-estrone or pasta e fagioli, do not rely on these small shapes for their pasta content but use some of the larger forms, from elbow macaroni to the finger-long and finger-thick pizzoccheri of the Valtellina. Stuffed pasta, too, is used in broth.

Fiochetti

Stellini

Conchigliette piccole

SHELLS & TWISTS

ITALIAN PASTA comes in a bewildering variety of shapes, whereas in middle Europe – from southern Germany and Switzerland to the Balkan countries – only the flat varieties we call 'noodles' and small soup pieces are traditional. Apart from the patterns dictated by finger movements, shapes have proliferated with the increase of commercial die-stamping.

The many corkscrew shapes, which in the home are made by twirling pasta around a knitting needle, or folding a strand in the middle and twisting it around itself (*gemelli*, 'twins'), are particularly effective to hold cheese and other sticky sauces.

Conchigliette

Conchiglie

Gnocchi

Farfalle

Fusilli

Riccioli

Funghini

Cappelletti

ITALIAN STUFFED PASTA

Tortellini

*S*TUFFED PASTA (pasta *ripiena*) *is always much better fresh than store-bought. It is made in many shapes and sizes, with a great variety of regional names – those above right are tortellini, or twists. There is no such thing as a traditional stuffing for any one shape, but Italian fillings tend to be savoury, whether using left-overs or resulting from pure fancy.*

Cappelletti

The round shapes sealed with a 'brim' of dough are usually called *cappelletti* (little hats) or *capelli di prete* (priests' hats). The larger variety of *capelli* is also called *orecchioni* (large ears). Many of the pasta names describe a basic shape. A variant, circular form of *tortellini* is made, like ravioli, from two pieces of *sfoglia* rather than by folding one piece in half.

Orecchioni

Round tortelloni

Small ravioli

Ravioli

As *tortelloni* are associated with Bologna and *cappelletti* with the central provinces in general, so ravioli are traditionally thought of as Genovese. The smaller ravioli often contain pork and beef, while larger ones have spinach and ricotta.

Agnolotti, from Piedmont, have a larger pasta edge than ravioli. They are made from a single piece of *sfoglia* folded over the filling.

Agnolotti

Square tortelloni

ORIENTAL PASTA

*A*LL OF ASIA *eats noodles. In the north they are usually made with wheat flour, while in the south rice flour predominates. There are also noodles made from mung bean starch, which have different properties: when deep-fried, they puff up and become crunchy; when soaked, they have a sponge-like capacity to absorb any sauce.*

Illustrated below are rice sticks and rice noodles. Rice sticks will break into short lengths when cooked; they can also be fried like bean threads. Rice noodles are best when fresh: the packet they come in should be supple. On the far right are two types of Chinese egg noodles. One is crinkly, the other plain. On the near right are three kinds of thin noodles or

vermicelli: at the top, two parcels of rice noodles; below those is a bundle of bean starch noodles which need only be soaked, but which can then withstand up to 20 minutes of braising without losing shape or texture; in the middle is a bundle of Japanese *somen*, a wheat flour noodle cooked while tied up, and eaten cold.

Rice sticks

Rice noodles

Rice noodles

Bean starch noodles

Crinkly egg noodles

Egg noodles

Somen

PASTA FROM CENTRAL & EASTERN EUROPE

*R*USSIA, POLAND, HUNGARY *and the Balkan countries use noodles, stuffed pasta and dumplings – either boiled or deep-fried – as staple foods. The Asian and Turkish invasions brought in dessert varieties with fruit, jam or other sweet fillings. Irregular pieces, grated from hard balls of egg-and-flour dough (above right) are known by various names:* Spätzle *in German,* tarhonya *in Hungarian and* zacierki *in Polish.*

Spätzle

The shapes of stuffed pasta are variants on folding a round or square piece of the basic sheet. Traditional Jewish *kreplach* (shown here, with the chicken liver filling of p. 35) is a square folded diagonally; the half-moon *pierogi* (on the opposite page) start as circles. Thimble dumplings (top right, opposite) are made from a double layer of dough, and puff into balls when fried.

Kreplach

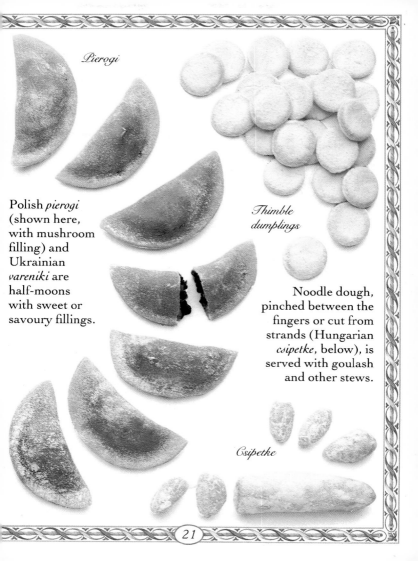

Pierogi

Thimble dumplings

Polish *pierogi* (shown here, with mushroom filling) and Ukrainian *vareniki* are half-moons with sweet or savoury fillings.

Noodle dough, pinched between the fingers or cut from strands (Hungarian *csipetke*, below), is served with goulash and other stews.

Csipetke

21

PASTA PARCELS

*T*HE DOUGH *for stuffed pasta has a flour, egg and water base, and it is often used both for a dumpling version and for 'skins' to wrap around different fillings. The resulting parcels can be either boiled or deep-fried. Boiling is done in water if the pasta is to accompany a dish, or in stock which will be served with the pasta.*

Vareniki

Manti

Manti are a Turkish and Armenian dish. They usually have a filling of minced meat with very subtle spicing – a recipe can be found on p. 38.

Vareniki are a speciality of the Ukraine. Their filling follows the seasons: cherries, berries, mushrooms, sauerkraut and preserves are used.

The fillings for these pasta parcels vary enormously according to what is locally available — seafood, meat, cheese and fruit are among the staple ingredients. The savoury versions are often served as snacks, or sold as street food, while sweet or fruit-filled varieties usually make a dessert. Meat, cheese and vegetable-filled parcels also go into stews.

Pel'meni

Wontons

Pel'meni from Siberia (served with a mustard and vinegar sauce there, a filling of greens in Central Asia) are sold throughout Russia in special cafés, *pel'mennaya*.

Wontons, common throughout China as deep-fried snacks (savoury, with a dip, or fruit-filled and sugared), are better known to us in soup.

Recipes

*All recipes are for 4
as a main course or for
6 as a starter*

FRESH PASTA

The basic proportions for
making fresh pasta are
3½ oz/100 g flour to 1 egg, but
the exact amount will vary
according to the flour and the
freshness and size of the eggs.
Commercial pasta is made with
flour from durum wheat, an
extremely hard flour which has a
high gluten content and requires
a lot of kneading. Strong white
bread flour combined with

unbleached plain flour is best for
home-made pasta.

*5 oz/150 g bread flour
5 oz/150 g plain flour
salt
3 eggs*

Mix together the two flours with
a good pinch of salt and make a
mound on a clean work surface.
Make a well in the middle and
break in the eggs. Beat the eggs

with a fork or mix with your fingers, drawing in the flour, a little at a time. Support the wall of flour with the other hand so that it doesn't collapse and allow the egg to run out. When you have a thick mixture, push in the remaining flour from the edges and work to a firm mass. It may still feel sticky, so sprinkle a little more flour on the surface and on your hands if necessary, and knead – push the ball of dough down and away from you with the heel of the hand, then double it over, give it a quarter turn and repeat the process. Knead for 5–8 minutes, until the dough is silky and elastic. Form it into a ball, cover with clingfilm or a cloth and leave to rest for an hour. If you want to leave it longer, put the covered dough in the refrigerator, but allow it to come back to room temperature before you work with it.

Making pasta in a food processor

Put the flour and salt into the machine and process briefly to blend. Lightly beat the eggs in a jug, turn on the machine and pour in the egg, a little at a time, through the feeder tube. Process until the mixture forms a compact ball. Remove the dough and knead briefly until it is smooth and elastic. Cover and leave to rest.

Green pasta

Parboil *6 oz/175 g spinach or chard leaves*, squeeze out all excess water and purée. Combine with the ingredients for the dough; mix the dough in a bowl if you are working by hand; add the purée to the egg if you use a food processor.

Herb pasta

Use a herb with a pronounced flavour, such as basil or parsley, or a mixture – tarragon, lovage, coriander, rocket, marjoram are all suitable. Chop *a good handful of herb leaves* finely and mix them into the dough.

Making pasta by hand

Divide the dough into 3, and roll each piece on a lightly floured surface, turning it at intervals to produce a round sheet. Do not push down on the rolling pin, but press the dough away from you, always rolling in one direction. When you can see the surface through the dough it is ready. Now leave it to dry for 20–30 minutes, until it looks dull and leathery.

To cut the pasta into ribbons, roll up the sheet of dough like a Swiss roll and cut across with a sharp knife. Cut fettuccine/tagliatelle 1/4 in/5 mm wide, linguine 1/8 in/3 mm. Unravel the ribbons and spread them on a lightly floured cloth. Leave to dry for 10 minutes before cooking.

For larger shapes or for stuffed pasta, cut the sheets on the work surface using a pasta wheel or knife.

Using a pasta machine

Make the dough as described, up to the kneading stage, kneading it just enough to bind it properly – the machine will do the rest. Divide the dough into 6 pieces, set the space between the rollers of the machine as wide as possible, flour the dough lightly and pass it through with one hand, turning the handle with the other. Fold the dough in 3 and put through the machine again. Repeat the process 5 or 6 times, to form a rectangle. Reduce the space between the rollers by 2 or 3 notches and feed through the sheet of dough. Reduce the space further and repeat. Now you will have a long sheet of dough which needs supporting as it comes out of the machine, or it will fold on itself and stick. Flour it lightly and leave to dry for 10 minutes over the back of a chair or clean garden canes supported at either end. Pass the dough through one of the cutting slots to get noodles of the width you require.

Keeping pasta

Fresh pasta is best used straight after it is made, but it can be left to dry for a little longer, covered with a cloth. It should still feel supple and leathery; if it becomes brittle, it is too dry.

Supple pasta can be put in an airtight plastic bag and kept in the refrigerator for 5–6 days, or it can be frozen.

Cooking pasta

Always cook pasta in plenty of boiling water, and test frequently to make sure it does not overcook. It should still be firm – al dente. Fresh linguine need only 2–3 minutes, spaghetti and fettuccine 3–5 minutes, depending on the thickness of the pasta.

For dry pasta, follow the instructions on the packet.

Rice Noodles with Pork and Crab

10 oz/300 g rice vermicelli
2 tablespoons soy sauce
1 tablespoon sherry
¹/₂ teaspoon chilli sauce
3 tablespoons oil
1 onion, sliced thinly
1 red pepper, sliced thinly
6 oz/175 g pork fillet,
cut in julienne strips
6 oz/175 g white crab meat, shredded
4 oz/125 g bean sprouts
2 tablespoons cashew nuts,
lightly toasted
2 tablespoons chopped coriander

Soak the noodles in warm water for 20 minutes. Blend together the soy sauce, sherry and chilli sauce and put aside. Heat the oil in a wok over high heat, put in the onion and red pepper and stir fry for 2 minutes. Add the pork and fry for a further 5 minutes, or until the pork is cooked. Put in the crab meat and bean sprouts and heat through. Drain the noodles and stir in with the nuts and coriander. Pour over the soy sauce mixture, toss and serve.

Stir-Fried Noodles with Mangetouts, Prawns and Mushrooms

12 oz/375 g Chinese flat noodles
2 tablespoons groundnut oil
a small piece of fresh ginger,
peeled and finely chopped
2–3 cloves garlic, finely chopped
12 oz/375 g mangetouts, trimmed
6 oz/175 g fresh shiitake
mushrooms, sliced, or 6 dried, soaked
for 20 minutes, drained and sliced
salt, soy sauce
3 spring onions, chopped
8 oz/250 g shelled prawns

Boil the noodles al dente, and whilst they are cooking heat the oil over a high heat in a wok. Add the ginger and garlic and stir fry for a minute, then add the mangetouts and mushrooms and season lightly with salt and soy sauce. Continue to stir fry for another 2–3 minutes, then add the spring onions and prawns. Add the drained noodles to the wok; toss and fry until some of the noodles are browning and the other ingredients are well distributed. Turn into a warm bowl and serve.

CHICKEN WITH NOODLES

This is a simple Japanese dish. Dashi granules or powder, which are mixed with water to make the stock, can be bought from Japanese shops, but a good chicken stock can be used instead.

12 oz/375 g udon or other wheat noodles
12 oz/375 g chicken breast, boned and skinned
1¹/₄ pints/725 ml dashi stock
4 tablespoons soy sauce
2 tablespoons sherry
1 teaspoon sugar
4 slices fresh ginger
6 spring onions, sliced thickly

Boil the noodles until tender, then drain and rinse in cold running water. Cut the chicken into small pieces. Put the dashi, soy sauce, sherry, sugar and ginger in a pan and bring to the boil. Add the chicken and simmer for 5–6 minutes, until it is done. Put in the onions and simmer a minute more. Reheat the noodles by pouring a kettle of boiling water over them. Divide them among 4 large warmed bowls. Ladle over the stock and arrange the chicken and onions on top.

LINGUINE WITH CORIANDER PESTO

a good sized bunch of coriander
4 tablespoons pine nuts
2 cloves garlic, crushed
4 tablespoons freshly grated parmesan
approx. ¹/₄ pint/150 ml olive oil
1 lb/500 g fresh linguine

Remove the stalks from the coriander and process or blend the leaves with the pine nuts, garlic and parmesan. Add the oil slowly whilst the machine is running. Scrape down the sides of the bowl with a spatula frequently to achieve a smooth sauce. Do not add too much oil; check the consistency as you work.
Put the pesto into a large warm bowl. Cook the pasta al dente, then drain and turn it into the bowl. Toss well to coat the pasta with the sauce and serve.

LINGUINE WITH PEAS AND WATERCRESS

2 bunches watercress
3 tablespoons olive oil
1 lb/500 g fresh small peas, podded
¼ pint/150 ml crème fraîche
salt and pepper
12 oz/350 g fresh linguine

Clean the watercress, remove any yellow leaves, tough stalks or whiskers and chop the rest. Heat the oil and fry the peas for 3–4 minutes, then add the watercress, crème fraîche, salt and pepper. Cook the sauce a little longer. Boil the linguine al dente, drain, mix with the sauce in a warm bowl, and serve.

FETTUCCINE WITH SWORDFISH

1 lb/500 g swordfish
2 cloves garlic, chopped
2 tablespoons lemon juice
4 tablespoons olive oil
salt and pepper
1 red pepper
2 large ripe tomatoes
12 oz/375 g fresh fettuccine
a handful of black olives,
stoned and chopped
chopped parsley

Cut the swordfish into bite-sized pieces and put it into an ovenproof dish with the garlic, lemon juice and 2 tablespoons olive oil. Season with salt and pepper. Toss well to coat the fish and marinate for 30 minutes. Put the pepper over a gas flame, or under a preheated grill, turning it occasionally until it is charred all over. Put it into a plastic bag and leave for a few minutes so that the steam loosens the skin.

Blanch the tomatoes in hot water for a few seconds and then peel them. Cut them into chunks and discard the seeds. Take the pepper out of the bag, remove skin, seeds and ribs and cut into thin strips. Put the fish and its marinade into a preheated oven, 200°C/400°F/gas 6, and bake for 10–12 minutes, until the pieces are just cooked through.

Cook the fettuccine al dente, drain and put into a warm bowl. Toss with the remaining oil. Add the fish and its liquid, the pepper, tomatoes, olives and parsley, toss carefully and serve.

SPAGHETTI WITH MUSSELS

2 lb/1 kg mussels
4–5 tablespoons olive oil
2 cloves garlic, chopped
1 medium can passata
1 bay leaf
a sprig of thyme
3 dried red chillies
salt and pepper
¼ pint/150 ml dry white wine
3 tablespoons finely chopped parsley
1 lb/500 g spaghetti

Clean the mussels and remove the beards. Discard any that are open or broken. Heat the oil in a large pan and sauté the garlic. Add the passata, bay leaf, thyme, chillies and season with salt and pepper. Simmer for 5 minutes then pour in the wine and bring to the boil. Put in the mussels and cover the pan. Shake it from time to time and continue cooking until the mussels are open. Any that fail to open should be thrown away. Remove most of the mussel shells and put the sauce to one side while the spaghetti cooks. Drain it well and turn it into a large bowl. Pour over the mussels and their sauce, garnish with parsley and serve.

SPAGHETTI ALLA CARBONARA

1 lb/500 g spaghetti
1 oz/25 g butter or 2 tablespoons
olive oil
4 oz/125 g lean bacon, diced
3 eggs
2 tablespoons grated parmesan
2 tablespoons grated pecorino
salt and pepper

Put the spaghetti to boil in plenty of salted water. Melt the butter in a large heavy pan and sauté the bacon until lightly coloured. Remove the pan from the heat and keep warm. Beat the eggs with half the cheese and season with lots of black pepper and a little salt. When the spaghetti is cooked, drain well and tip it into the pan with the bacon. Do not put the pan back on the heat; pour in the egg mixture and toss thoroughly so that all the pasta is coated with the mixture. Sprinkle over the remaining cheese and serve at once on very hot plates.

FUSILLI WITH MONKFISH

2 carrots
1 small bulb fennel
2 courgettes
4 tablespoons olive oil
1 lb/500 g monkfish, cut in cubes
3 tablespoons dry white wine
salt and pepper
10 oz/300 g fusilli
2 tablespoons chopped parsley

Cut the vegetables into matchstick pieces. Heat 3 tablespoons oil in a pan and sauté them for 4–5 minutes, stirring frequently. Remove the vegetables and keep warm. Add the monkfish to the pan, sauté for a few minutes, then pour over the wine, season with salt and pepper, cover and simmer for 5–6 minutes. Put the vegetables back in the pan and cook for a further 5 minutes. While preparing the sauce, cook the pasta in plenty of salted boiling water. Drain well and toss with the last spoonful of oil. Spoon the fish and vegetables and their juices over the pasta, toss carefully, sprinkle with parsley and serve.

SPAGHETTI ALLA PUTTANESCA

12 oz/375 g spaghetti
6 tablespoons olive oil
3 cloves garlic, chopped finely
1 red chilli pepper, chopped
6 anchovy fillets, chopped
1 lb/500 g ripe tomatoes,
peeled and chopped
4 oz/125 g large black olives, stoned
1 tablespoon capers
salt

Cook the spaghetti in a large pan of boiling water while you make the sauce. Heat the oil in a frying pan and fry the garlic and chilli until the garlic starts to brown. Add the anchovy fillets and mash them with a fork. Now put in the tomatoes, olives and capers. Mix well, taste to see if salt is needed and simmer until the spaghetti is ready. Drain the pasta, put it in a large warm bowl and pour over the sauce.

PENNE WITH BROAD BEANS AND ASPARAGUS

8 oz/250 g asparagus
12 oz/375 g shelled broad beans
3–4 tablespoons olive oil
1 onion, chopped
4 oz/125 g pancetta or bacon,
chopped
salt and pepper
12 oz/375 g penne
basil leaves
pecorino cheese

Remove any tough stalks from the asparagus and cut it into short lengths. Cook in boiling salted water for 2–3 minutes only, so that it is still crisp, then drain. Boil the beans for 8–10 minutes and drain. Heat the oil and sauté the onion. When it has wilted, add the pancetta and after 3–4 minutes, the cooked asparagus and beans. Taste for seasoning. Cook the penne, drain and stir into the sauce. Serve topped with torn basil leaves together with grated pecorino cheese.

PASTA AND VEGETABLE STEW

4 oz/125 g haricot beans,
soaked overnight
3/4 pint/450 ml chicken stock
1 potato, cubed
2 carrots, sliced
2 stalks celery, sliced
2 leeks, sliced
2 courgettes, sliced
4 oz/125 g cabbage, shredded
3 oz/75 g shelled peas
2 tomatoes, peeled and chopped
2 tablespoons chopped fresh herbs –
thyme, marjoram, savory
salt and pepper
8 oz/250 g rigatoni
1 tablespoon olive oil
parmesan cheese

Cook the haricot beans until almost tender, about 30 minutes. Bring the chicken stock to the boil in a large pan and put in the potato, carrots, celery and leeks. Cook over high heat for 5 minutes, then add the remaining vegetables, including the drained beans, and the herbs. Season with salt and pepper and simmer steadily for a further 8–10 minutes. Cook the rigatoni, drain and toss in the oil, then add to the stew. Serve with grated parmesan cheese.

HUNGARIAN CABBAGE AND NOODLES

A surprisingly good dish often served at the end of the meal in Hungarian restaurants. The noodle squares must predominate, with shreds of cabbage among them.

fresh pasta (see recipe, p.24)
1 small green cabbage,
shredded finely
1 teaspoon sugar
2 oz/50 g lard or butter
salt and paprika

Sprinkle salt on the cabbage and leave to drain for 20 minutes. Make the dough, roll it out and cut into 1 in/2.5 cm squares.

Press the liquid from the cabbage, then sauté with the sugar in the lard in a large pan, stirring well. Boil the noodle squares in salted water until just cooked. Drain and add them to the cabbage. Toss to coat them well in the fat. Sprinkle with paprika and serve.

KREPLACH FILLED WITH CHICKEN LIVERS

A traditional Jewish dish usually served at festivals.

fresh pasta (see recipe, p.24)
12 oz/350 g chicken livers
1 oz/25 g chicken fat or butter
1 onion, chopped
yolks of 2 hard boiled eggs
3 tablespoons chopped parsley
salt and pepper

Make the pasta and roll it out thinly. While it is drying prepare the filling. Sauté the livers in the fat for 6–8 minutes. Let them cool slightly, then put through a mincer with the other ingredients. Season and cool completely. Cut the pasta into 2 in/5 cm squares. Put a teaspoon of filling on each one, wet the edges of the dough lightly and fold over to form a triangle. Press the edges together firmly.

Cook the kreplach in boiling water or stock, not too many at a time – they should not be crowded. Simmer for 8–10 minutes, or until they rise to the surface. If you cook the kreplach in stock, serve them with the stock in soup plates; if they are cooked in water, drain and pour melted butter over them.

BEAN AND PASTA SALAD

4 oz/125 g flageolets
4 oz/125 g haricot beans
6 oz/175 g shells or bows
4 oz/125 g French beans
1 clove garlic, chopped
a handful of chopped fresh herbs –
rocket, parsley, tarragon, chives,
basil, chervil
6 tablespoons olive oil
2 tablespoons wine vinegar
1 teaspoon mustard
salt and pepper

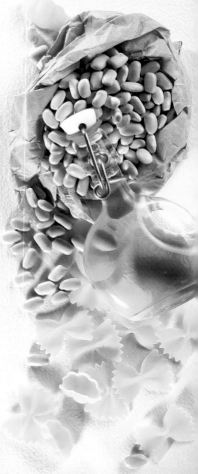

Soak the dried beans separately
for a few hours, then boil them
until just tender. Drain, rinse in
cold water and put aside. Cook
the pasta just al dente, drain and
refresh in cold water too. Top
and tail the French beans, boil
briefly, drain and cool.
Combine the beans, pasta, garlic
and herbs in a large bowl. Make
a sharp dressing with the
remaining ingredients. Pour it
over the salad and toss carefully.
Chill for an hour or two
before serving.

BAKED SHELLS WITH SPINACH AND RICOTTA

10 oz/300 g pasta shells
8 oz/250 g spinach
8 oz/250 g ricotta
1/4 pint/150 ml single cream
1/2 teaspoon ground cinnamon
salt and pepper
3 tablespoons grated parmesan
1 oz/25 g butter

Cook the pasta shells in boiling water. Blanch the spinach in boiling water for 1 minute, drain, refresh in cold water and squeeze dry. Put the spinach into a processor with the ricotta, cream, cinnamon, salt and pepper and purée. Drain the shells and mix them with the spinach purée. Pour into a buttered gratin dish, scatter grated parmesan over the top, dot with butter and cover with foil. Bake in a preheated oven, 180°C/350°F/gas 4, for 15 minutes, then remove the foil and return to the oven to brown for 5 minutes.

BOWS WITH SMOKED TROUT AND ROCKET

10 oz/300 g bows
6 tablespoons olive oil
1 small cucumber
2 smoked trout, skinned, filleted and boned
1 bunch small radishes
3–4 large handfuls of rocket leaves
lemon juice
salt and pepper
horseradish cream (optional)

Cook the bows, drain, rinse in cold water, drain again, then toss in a large bowl with 4 tablespoons olive oil. Cut the cucumber in half lengthways, discard the seeds and cut into small wedges. Sprinkle with salt and leave to drain for 15 minutes. Cut the fish into bite-sized pieces. Top and tail the radishes and leave whole. Tear the rocket leaves into 2 or 3 pieces if they are very large. Rinse the cucumber and dry with kitchen paper.

Make a sharp dressing with the remaining oil, lemon juice, salt and pepper and a little horseradish if desired. Add the fish and vegetables to the pasta, pour over the dressing, toss gently and serve.

Manti

Small pasta parcels, cooked in varying ways, are found throughout central Asia, from Chinese wontons to these richly flavoured mantı from Turkey.

7 oz/200 g plain flour
salt
2 eggs
2–3 tablespoons water (if necessary)
8 oz/250 g minced lamb
1 onion, chopped finely
2 tablespoons chopped parsley
2 teaspoons paprika
³/₄ pint/450 ml stock
3 cloves garlic
¹/₂ pint/300 ml thick yogurt
2 oz/50 g butter
¹/₄ teaspoon dried mint

Make a stiff dough with flour, salt, eggs and water, following the instructions on p.24. Cover and leave to rest for 30 minutes. Roll out thinly and cut into 2 in/5 cm squares. Mix together the lamb, onion, parsley and seasonings. Put a teaspoon of the filling in the centre of each square, then wet the edges lightly and join the two opposite corners of the square. Bring up the other two corners and pinch all four together in a point, to make a star-shaped parcel. Put the mantı in a single layer in a buttered ovenproof dish and bake in a preheated oven, 200°C/400°F/gas 6, for 20–25 minutes, until they are golden. Heat the stock, pour it over the mantı, cover the dish and return it to the oven for 15 minutes. Crush the garlic with salt and beat it into the yogurt. Pour it over the mantı. Melt the butter, stir in the mint and pour over the yogurt. Serve in bowls.

RAVIOLI FILLED WITH SAFFRON RICOTTA

fresh pasta (see recipe, p.24)
12 oz/375 g ricotta
1/4 teaspoon saffron
1 tablespoon milk
grated rind of 1 orange
1 egg
nutmeg
salt and pepper
4 oz/125 g butter
fresh sage or rosemary leaves
2 slices prosciutto, cut in strips
(optional)

Make the pasta and divide it into 2 pieces. Roll out thinly into 2 rectangles of equal size. Soak the saffron in the milk for 20 minutes, then mix it into the ricotta with the orange rind, egg, some freshly grated nutmeg and salt and pepper to taste.

Put olive-sized portions of the filling on one sheet of pasta, in lines about 1 1/2 in/3.5 cm apart. Place the other sheet on top and press down between the rows of filling. Cut between the rows with a sharp knife or a pasta wheel to form squares of ravioli. Press the edges together to make sure they are sealed. Leave to stand while you bring a large pot of salted water to the boil. Cook the ravioli until they puff up slightly, about 5 minutes. Drain carefully and toss in the melted butter flavoured with a few sage leaves or chopped rosemary leaves and, if you wish, a few strips of prosciutto.

INDEX

ACKNOWLEDGEMENTS

*The publishers
would like to thank
the following*

· TYPESETTING ·
TRADESPOOLS LTD
FROME

PHOTOGRAPHIC
· ASSISTANCE ·
JONATHAN BUCKLEY

JACKET
· PHOTOGRAPHY ·
DAVE KING

· ILLUSTRATOR ·
JANE THOMSON

· REPRODUCTION ·
COLOURSCAN
SINGAPORE

PAGE 5 F.LLI DE CECCO DI FILIPPO, ITALY PAGE **27** MARY EVANS PICTURE LIBRARY, LONDON
PAGE **31** THE MANSELL COLLECTION, LONDON

GWEN EDMONDS FOR ADDITIONAL HELP · LOUISE PICKFORD FOR PREPARING FOOD
KARL SHONE FOR PHOTOGRAPHY ON PAGES 20-3

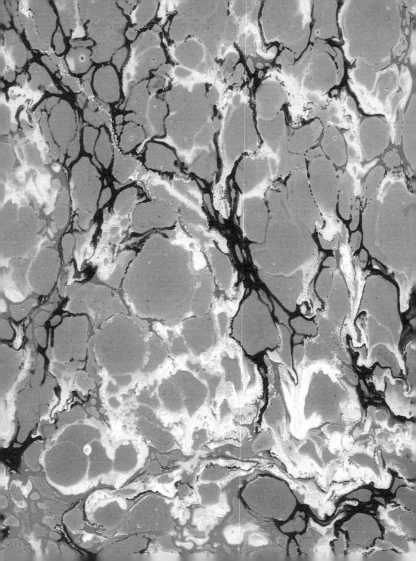